MW00872895

This Early Dark

Micropoetry and ultra-flash fiction

Michael Cadnum

for Sherina

street to street, dawn to dawn

Horse Eagle Press

Acknowledgments

Some of the writing in this collection has appeared in the following publications:

America Literary On-line, *American Tanka*, *Blue Unicorn*, *Bottle Rockets*, *Modern Haiku*, *Rolling Stone*, and *The Virginia Quarterly Review*

Jacket photo Arianne Hastings

My thanks to Don Morgan for suggesting this book, and for his advice and comments during the writing.

My thanks, too, for Vigdis Storsletten for her advice and insight.

And to Adam Friedlander for his patient help.

Table of Contents

6

1

Quiet noon, birds asleep, a truck turning the
corner driven by no one

A hole in the lake. The woman not knowing
she's sad.

You send me a picture of your hand. I touch the
screen.

If you're depressed all the time, she said, rolling down the window, grief is not a shock.

After the first one, there will always be a spider.

Eel River, first vacation, where I forgot what my mother looked like, and I found the suitcase full of rain.

9

He sold the Indian four-cylinder, the Harley that gave him the road rash, and the BMW he shot the guy stealing.

Hot weather again. The vicar naked in the motel by the manmade lake.

This is not a mystery, but it is a secret.

She didn't turn on her web cam, so he talked to the blank.

A book blown open and stuck

The miller laughed soundlessly, all those seasons of chaff.

11

An old letter from you—I close my eyes to read the rest.

The cloud, the shadow of the cloud on the mountain

12

2

I cannot bring myself to break the skin of this
orange, warm from your touch

We learned the local dialect, the moue that meant
no, and the baby talk that ordered men into
chains.

A windy night, the street empty, except for the
priest retrieving spilled firewood.

Only when it's gone does the passing jet whisper.

I have not heard from you for so long you sit in every room

I answer the question you never asked a little better each time

I thought you touched me but it was the rain

Soapsuds across the carpet where you left the bath to watch him leave

The tiny blue vein in the eyelid of the woman reading braille

Dark cat come lap this full moon.

Foggy morning—you have to trust the world to remember

The Ferris wheel's creaking stillness while the earth falls

Voices made lovely by distance

The fog lifts, along with some of the trees

I was tired until I saw the sparrow, feathers
fanned to pleasure in the dust

Infant in the park, his wail starting milk in the
breasts of strangers

A rat on the fire escape, pouring his body
carefully down

His mother was a pianist. There were no pianos.

In the crowded airport before you embrace,
before you kiss, you reach to take her burden.

Daylight shaken-out and let fall soundlessly over
her sleep.

tall grasses
beyond the laughter
of the unwanted guest

I make a doll of paper bags, paper stuffing, ink smile, but never, never will I give it eyes.

Sometimes when I'm writing I hold my breath and only breathe again as someone new.

If we could stay like this--
dawn rain
my neighbor
trying forever to
start his car.

Lean into me again and say we're dancing.

Lighting cigarettes, windy night, golden hands.

How lovely, the wrinkled tablecloth now that
everyone's gone

22

3

Deer return to the dry lake and drink the cold air.

My grandfather rises early in the pre-dawn cold, and lights a fire. Long after he's gone he warms his hands.

She draws a star. She draws another star, and another. She takes forever.

Years after the cat is gone shadows everywhere
wash themselves.

The mare remembers you and ambles over,
bringing along with her the world

How can I be sad when there's a child being a
horse in the Target parking lot?

Still no snow--
my letter to you blank

The flock of starlings flying off the roof keep the
shape of the house

I am watching when the streetlights come on—a
mild shock, like the apology of an angry man.

I hold my breath through the shadow of your house.

Panicked sparrow in the laundromat—only when he's exhausted can I feel his heartbeat.

She plaits her hair so he can take it down: she knows it won't last.

Shake it to the east and shake it to the west, teach
that dog to bark

Midnight, out-of-hock Gretsch round-badge
dazzling, backbeat, hi-hat, landlord tiki-head
mad.

I will not mention the softly singing pregnant
woman, digging up last year's tomato vines

Lying under the blanket beside you as though we will always

I drew a picture of you gone. It is a picture of you almost here.

A lake so deep it darkens the sun.

Once everything in her kingdom was free, but you had to kill for it.

4

As I put on my white stockings my toe finds a hole only you will see

All that season I tried to be something a hummingbird would touch with his tongue

Hot afternoon, crows with their black beaks soothe each other's wings.

The curtains blowing, open window, what I
believe

Heavy with peaches the falling branch wakes us
both

She had a Peavey amp and a Gibson four-string,
walking bass counter to the hungry noon

I found your cigarettes in the suitcase and wake
with your cough.

The dream again, the blue dress, everyone glad to
see you.

Why anything? Why not just the yellow kitchen,
blue cup on the sink?

Pour that concrete and smooth it so the cat cat cat.

Nanny on two legs, two legs, two legs, let that baby sleep.

Boat across the bay. Friend around the world. Blessed cat, who cannot guess.

The first doves, ash-blue wings, this and this and this.

The mirror and the room, so still

After dark I wish I had not cut off so many branches.

The quiet is broken—a neighbor's dog lapping water under the porch-light.

Endless work, trout swimming to stay in the shade.

I run on this and I run on that, I'm the lizard in my too-tight (way too) skin.

With you again in the empty room.

I don't step into the same river twice, I step into it forever.

Short daylight. Long dark. Tear here.

She scribbled grass. She scribbled more grass.
Erased you a path.

The black coat hanging on the door? Oh, it's
been there forever.

Living waters, the coyote drinking from the pond
even when he's gone.

39

5

Why is the air so cold right here in front of your mirror?

It doesn't move--the shadow of the branch on the waves.

I burn the words to make them happen.

The shoe does not know there's another.

My starched shirt whispers as I straighten the photo of your smile.

Deer graze in the horses' shadows. Do I often think of you?

Again I learn the words of your beautiful
language and forget them hill by hill.

Your laugh more and more mine

Hot night, no ice, screen door claw-holes where
the gone cat climbed.

I'm painting the window, I'm painting the window frame, so when you cruise that avenue you'll see that I'm not here.

Summer night the shore-leave pickpockets chugging triple sec.

I wake, and then I really wake. This was the door until they bricked it.

I built a tower. The tower had a shadow. I lived
in the shadow with you.

How she smiles when she sees me, the woman
who lied.

She didn't want to know
who the father was,
fingering the knot in her scarf.

Dawn, fresh graffiti on the bread truck.

The man who sold mechanical birds
in the park not waking one morning
and selling the birds just the same.

The laughing boy in a yellow shirt jumps up and
down outside the tractor shed.

Inside the rain is rain. Outside the rain is the
heron.

With care I avoid staring
into the blind woman's face.

The laugh down the hall. The rented morning.
She remembers having wings.

I looked for you but all I saw was a slim, weary woman with a child.

I realize the book is reading me and I close it.

6

An atheist among the gods in my new red socks I
kiss you

The truth of my room at sunset
is that darkness touches
also your absence.

The brushing of cockleburs, softly, between us
that mercy.

She holds the empty cup and looks out through
the door for the moon.

Frankie & Johnny

Lick the truth like a smoke
deep sleeper
shoot your cuffs on the endless street
stride smooth bright whisper
while all these midnights
Frankie cries

The Pit

Father buried us to our heads.
How do we look we called.
Come back we called.
And we laughed though the weight
made it hard,
come back, come back
the foam at our lips tasting of keys and nails
melting at our breath.

She is drawing
on the far side of night
so be careful
Cat-of-Stars
with your blue planet

All the way up the hill
I protect the junk mail
from the wind.

At One Point

At one point the word had
gotten out that I was
interested in human remains.
This lead, I must say, to the worst
experiences of my life.

This early darkness makes us laugh in whispers.

Yellow eyes of blackbirds, the big closed book of earth.

Now I am happy, she thinks, the family home, the potato eyes freshly gouged.

She leaves the door open, mistaking the
neighbor's new electric fire for the moon.

The cat trilling through her nose for the kittens
we gave away

The blackbird on the high voltage line, singing
even when he's not.

No fish in the new fishpond, the gardener soaking his feet

She used to love him, but now she lives with the tide schedule pinned by a knife.

Cattle on the hill—when did they all turn from the rain?

57

7

The woman with three cats yelling angrily at the
children.

From all the way across the river the dog
watching me wags his tail.

Awake early I tiptoe through the pearls where
your necklace broke

The old, rippled window panes gently slicing
passing traffic

The chime of her earrings she takes everything
off.

When there is no dragon—that's exactly when.
Nope, no dragon=dragon's back again.

I never speak of you
but sometimes when you're on my mind
she asks why I'm smiling.

This is obvious he said pointing at nothing

Canyon road dry, shadow wet sun

A single reed alive within the sinews of the
basket

The gun dogs asleep
garage door open
the poacher loading the freezer

The bear bearded
with millrace ice
eyes my dog

The bear does not
watch the heron
until she's gone

Empty shipyard
milkweed to the sea

A distal fracture
says the doctor,
pointing down the broken road.

Where you are quiet the quiet is yours

Until every course a life can take is either a
search or a vigil

The green field and the magpie—even when the
magpie flies away.

All day no birds in the new birdbath.

Into our dry sunlight rolls the freight train
glistening with rain.

I'm the whale, swallowed Jonah, coughed him
up, toured the clubs, played the Strip, hooked bad
to the long-gone runaway

In the end we forgive, the long stairway, the taxis
in the rain

Cigarette you exhale, talking dirty.

She sleeps on the prairie but dreams of the sea

I'm never going home you say streetlight to
streetlight, almost there

Let's not play that game again where I walk the
bridge and try to see you waving.

How bright this rainy night the bus with no passengers.

Michael Cadnum is the author of thirty-five
books, both fiction and poetry, including *Saint
Peter's Wolf* and the National Book Award
Finalist *The Book of the Lion*. *This Early Dark*
presents micro-poetry and ultra-flash fiction
written over a forty-year period, and brings to
further life Cadnum's fascination with desire and
discovery.

Cadnum knocks us off our platitudes and sends
us sliding elsewhere...and we are smoothly swept
into a new field of perception.

Ted Kooser, *The Georgia Review*

Made in the USA
Coppell, TX
02 March 2020